God is the beginning
And the ending of all things.
It is He who gives us life
From the beggar to the king.

Long before the world existed
There was God upon His throne,
Surrounded by His angels
In His perfect golden home.

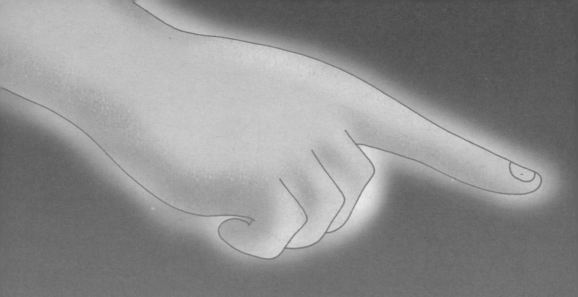

'Twas there the Lord decided,
In the glory that is His,
To set about creating
Everything that was and is.

So it was in the beginning
God made the heavens and the earth.
In such amazing glory
Was our whole world given birth.

TURN PAGE

DAY ONE

Everything was darkness when
God said, "Let there be light!"
And He called this brightness day.
And He called the darkness night.

TURN PAGE

DAY TWO

Then the Lord created earth
And made it spin around.
And placed above a wondrous sky
Just like a big blue crown.

TURN
PAGE

DAY THREE
And the Lord did cover earth
With oceans deep and wide.
How they splashed in mighty waves
As they rolled from side to side.

Up from these great, vast oceans
God then made the land appear,
All the mountains and the plains
That stretch from there to here.

TURN PAGE

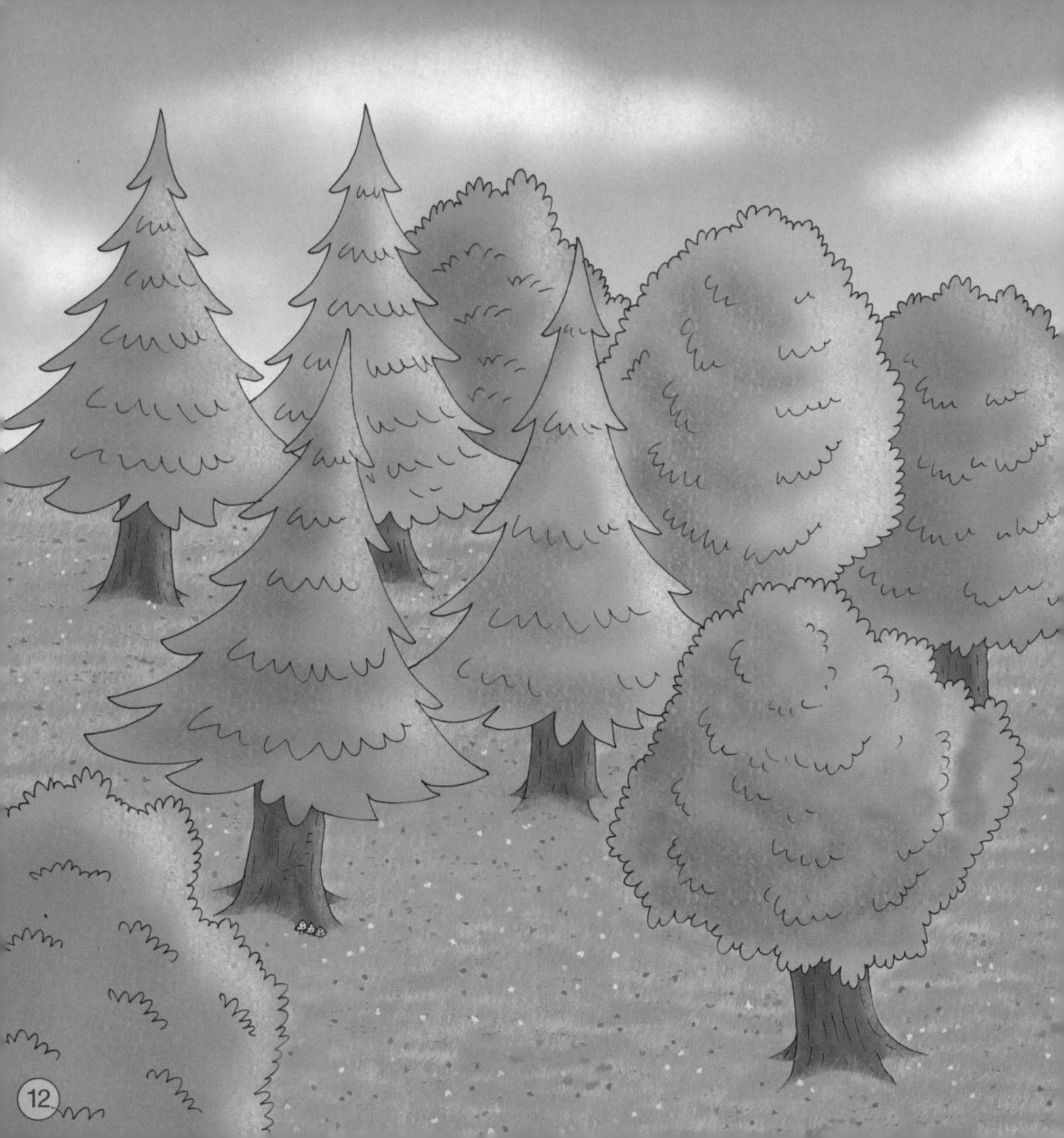

All across this newborn land
God created grass and trees,
And a rainbow burst of flowers
That did sway upon the breeze.

TURN PAGE

DAY FOUR

Then did God create the sun
To make the daytime warm.
For night, the moon and twinkling stars
By His grace were formed.

TURN PAGE

14

DAY FIVE
Now the Lord did fill the seas
With every kind of fish,
And crabs and turtles, dolphins, too,
All things that splash and splish.

TURN PAGE

17

And then God filled the skies with life,
The birds of flight and feather.
Oh, how they filled the world with song
As they all chirped together.

DAY SIX
Then God created animals
With horns and tooth and fur,
The buffalo and elephants
And cats that meow and purr.

At last the Lord created
Man and woman, too.
From them come every one of us
Including me and you

DAY SEVEN
After all had been created
God took the seventh day,
And made it one of peace and rest
To give us time to pray.

For all we have and all we know,
Let's give thanks to the Lord.
Let's thank Him for our precious earth
And His endless reward.